SHAKESPEARE LEGENDS ALPHABET

William Shakespeare (1564–1616) wrote poetry and plays of an amazing power and variety. He is considered the most influential writer in English literature history. His plays continue to be translated, adapted, performed, studied and read throughout the world more than 400 years after his death.

Words by Robin Feiner & Mary Barnes Jenkins

A is for **A**riel.
Imprisoned in a tree by
a witch, then bound in service
to Prospero the magician
who releases him, this airy
spirit longs to be free. But
first he must use his invisibility
and magic against Prospero's
enemies. Ariel causes the
'tempest' that gives
Shakespeare's legendary
play its name.

B is for Nick **B**ottom. Rehearsing a play in the forest with other workingmen on a Midsummer Night, this humble weaver is transformed into a donkey by a mischievous fairy. After a night of magical revelry with the fairy queen, Bottom wakes in human form, describing the "most rare vision" of his wonderful dream.

C is for Caliban.
Wild, earthy and ignorant, Caliban was abandoned by his witch mother to grow up alone on a deserted island. When, in Shakespeare's 'The Tempest,' a magician and his daughter are shipwrecked there, they try to educate and civilize Caliban, but he remains angry, undisciplined and fierce.

D is for **D**esdemona. Without her father's consent, she marries Othello, a man from a different race and culture. She then leaves the protection of her family to follow her new husband to war, remaining noble, faithful and trusting, even in the face of adversity.

E is for **E**dmund.
As an illegitimate son, he resents that he will never inherit his noble father's property or title. Clever and attractive, and caring only about himself, he will do anything to succeed, no matter how much suffering he causes his own family and the royal family of King Lear.

F is for John **F**alstaff.
This aging knight, large in figure and personality, curries favor with young Prince Hal in hopes of reward when Hal becomes king. Falstaff shows Hal how ordinary people live, but Hal knows his friendship with the debauched and dishonest Falstaff cannot continue once he ascends the throne.

G is for Queen Gertrude. Upon her husband's death, Gertrude's son Hamlet should have become king. But her hurried marriage to Hamlet's uncle gives Claudius the throne instead. She tries to make peace between her son and new husband, but she is troubled by her role in the turbulent events in the Danish court.

H is for Hamlet.
When his father's ghost demands revenge, this young prince swears to kill his father's brother and murderer, King Claudius. Hamlet struggles with his conscience, wondering if he is doing the right thing, famously questioning his resolution "to be or not to be."

I is for **I**ago.
Passed over for a promotion,
ambitious Iago pretends
to be a faithful and honest
servant to General Othello.
But admitting "I am not what
I am," Iago creates a complex
lie that makes an embroidered
handkerchief, innocently lost,
seem to Othello like proof
of his wife's infidelity.

Jj

J is for Juliet, and her Romeo. At a masked ball in fair Verona, Juliet meets Romeo, son of her family's enemies. Exchanging lovers' vows on a moonlit balcony, and then secretly marrying, they are soon separated by ill-fated events in this epic tale of star-crossed lovers.

K is for **K**atherine the Shrew. Criticized for loudly expressing her strong opinions, Kate meets her match when her father marries her to Petruchio. In the skirmish between two intense personalities, husband and wife learn to win and lose, and in the end both are tamed by respect and affection.

L is for King **L**ear.
This aging king rashly divides his kingdom between two flattering daughters, and unfairly banishes the third, who truly loves him. Blinded by his own selfishness, Lear makes a tragic journey into madness, but learns to feel genuine *sympathy* for the suffering of others.

Mm

M is for **M**acbeth, and his Lady. After witches predict he will be king hereafter, Macbeth desires the crown but hesitates to murder the king to gain the throne. His ambitious wife provides the cool and unnatural determination to do whatever is necessary to achieve power.

N is for Nurse to Juliet. She never uses one word when 10 will do! Since Juliet's birth, Nurse has cared for her "ladybird" and loved her like her own daughter. But ignoring the hatred between their parents' families, Nurse helps arrange the secret wedding of her Juliet to Romeo.

O is for **O**thello.
Having overcome great
hardship and proving himself
in battle, this Moorish general
is chosen to defend Venice.
However, Othello's legendary
vulnerability is the intense
love he feels for his new wife,
Desdemona. "She loved me
for the dangers I had passed,
and I loved her that she did
pity them."

P is for Prospero.
Banished and finding refuge
on an isolated island, Prospero
uses magic to dominate his
daughter, Miranda, and
two otherworldly creatures
he finds there. By the end
of 'The Tempest,' he discards
the magic that he used to
control others, finally under-
standing that "we are such
stuff as dreams are made on."

Q is for **Q**ueen Cleopatra. Intelligent, ruthless and undeniably attractive, she rules ancient Egypt and enchants Roman general, Mark Antony. His passionate choice, to abandon his family and military ambitions in Rome to follow her, leads them both to tragic personal and political loss.

R is for King Richard III. Born deformed, and claiming to feel neither pity, love nor fear, Richard becomes king by committing murder and using his surprisingly effective charm. He dies in battle when forced to fight on foot, crying: "A horse! A horse! My kingdom for a horse!"

S is for Shylock.
A Jew and an outsider,
Shylock lends money to
Venetian merchants who
publically humiliate him.
But he and his enemies
share good and bad human
qualities: "If you prick us
do we not bleed? If you
tickle us do we not laugh?
And if you wrong us shall
we not revenge?"

T is for **T**itania.
After this beautiful, stubborn fairy queen clashes with her husband, he uses a magic flower to make her fall in love with the next thing she sees: a humble weaver transformed into a donkey! At daylight, the magic dissolves, the fairy couple is reconciled, and Titania wakes from her embarrassing dream.

U is for **U**rsula.
As a gentlewoman working in a wealthy household, clever Ursula conspires with her mistress and her friends to trick two stubborn people into admitting their love for each other. In 'Much Ado about Nothing,' everyone plays at love, as "some Cupid kills with arrows, some with traps."

Vv

V is for **V**iola. Shipwrecked alone in a strange country, she disguises herself as a boy, Cesario, for her own protection. In the comedy, 'Twelfth Night,' Viola soon discovers that, male or female, love tends to encourage a lot of very foolish behavior.

W is for the **W**itches. Three weird sisters chant, recite spells, and brew odd recipes in their cauldron. "Double, double, toil and trouble!" On a deserted battlefield, they address Macbeth and Banquo, exhausted warriors, predicting royal futures for both men. What will these men do to make those prophecies real?

X is for Polixenes.
After being falsely accused of betraying his lifelong friend, King Leontes, Polixenes escapes to his own kingdom to avoid being murdered. Their extraordinary friendship ends bitterly, but time passes, and their children provide a happy ending to 'The Winter's Tale.'

Yy

Y is for Yorick.
Yorick was the court jester
when Prince Hamlet was
a boy. When a gravedigger
unearths Yorick's skull,
Hamlet marvels that someone
once so full of life and laughter
has come to this end: "Alas,
poor Yorick, I knew him ...
A fellow of infinite jest, of most
excellent fancy."

Z is for Florizel.
When Prince Florizel falls in love with Perdita, his father, King Polixenes, forbids their marriage because she is but a shepherdess and a commoner. But Shakespeare's 'The Winter's Tale' ends warmly, when it is discovered that Perdita also has royal blood.

The ever-expanding legendary library

EXPLORE THESE LEGENDARY ALPHABETS & MORE AT WWW.ALPHABETLEGENDS.COM

SHAKESPEARE LEGENDS ALPHABET
www.alphabetlegends.com

Published by Alphabet Legends Pty Ltd in 2020
Created by Beck Feiner
Copyright © Alphabet Legends Pty Ltd 2020

978-0-6486724-6-3